Dyke and Sparhawk

The Acts and Resolutions Adopted by the General Assembly of Florida,

At its Thirteenth Session, Begun and Held at the Capitol, in the City of Tallahassee, on Monday, November 21st, 1864

Dyke and Sparhawk

The Acts and Resolutions Adopted by the General Assembly of Florida,
At its Thirteenth Session, Begun and Held at the Capitol, in the City of Tallahassee, on Monday, November 21st, 1864

ISBN/EAN: 9783337184568

Printed in Europe, USA, Canada, Australia, Japan

Cover: Foto ©Suzi / pixelio.de

THE
ACTS AND RESOLUTIONS

ADOPTED BY THE

GENERAL ASSEMBLY OF FLORIDA,

AT ITS

THIRTEENTH SESSION,

BEGUN AND HELD AT THE CAPITOL, IN THE CITY OF TALLAHASSEE, ON MONDAY, NOVEMBER 21ST, 1864.

PUBLISHED BY AUTHORITY OF LAW,
UNDER THE DIRECTION OF THE ATTORNEY GEOERAL.

TALLAHASSEE:
OFFICE OF THE FLORIDIAN & JOURNAL.
PRINTED BY DYKE & SPARHAWK.

1865.

TITLES

OF

ACTS AND RESOLUTIONS

PASSED BY THE

First Session of the Thirteenth General Assembly,

1864.

An act to create special tribunals for the trial of capital offences committed by slaves, free negroes and mulattoes.

An act to amend an act entitled an act to establish and permanently locate the county site of Manatee county, approved Dec. 5, 1861.

An act to repeal an act entitled "an act to consolidate the offices of Clerk of the Circuit Court and Judge of Probate in and for Manatee county," approved December 8, 1862.

An act to organize militia troops for the State of Florida.

An act to amend the laws relating to slaves.

An act relating to the accounts of Ex-Governor M. S. Perry and H. V. Snell, late Quarter-Master General.

An act relative to holding Commissioners' Courts of Lafayette county.

An act to amend an act entitled "an act for the protection of cattle owners in the counties of Levy, Lafayette, Taylor, Wakulla and Duval," approved November 27, 1863.

An act for the relief of our sick and wounded soldiers.

An act to provide for the appointment of county officers in certain cases.

An act to authorize William F. Russell to enter one hundred and sixty acres of land.

An act to provide for taking the census in the year 1865, in this State.

An act to amend "an act to provide for the establishment of two Seminaries of Learning."

An act for the education of soldiers' children.

An act to amend an act entitled "an act to allow the Supreme Court of this State to hold extra terms in certain cases therein specified," approved December 28, 1854.

An act to fix the county site of Brevard county, and for other purposes.

An act to facilitate the transaction of business in the Quarter-Master General's Office.

An act in relation to estates in this State.

An act to increase the price of Public Lands.

An act to amend the laws providing for the stay of executions.

An act to amend "an act to incorporate the city of Lake City."

An act to authorize the administrator of the estate of Anna L. Casey to make titles to certain lots in Columbia county.

An act in relation to the commissions of executors, guardians, curators and administrators.

An act to amend an act entitled "an act to amend the election laws of this State as regards the mode of voting, and for other purposes," approved December 8, 1862.

An act to appropriate a fund for clothing of troops from Florida in the Confederate service, and to purchase and distribute cards.

An act relative to the fees of the Clerk of the Supreme Court and Jailors.

An act in relation to the public defence.

An act to protect the citizens of Florida.

An act for the relief of C. L. Demilly.

An act to extend the term of the Solicitors in the several Judicial Circuits in this State to the first day of January, 1866, and for other purposes.

An act in relation to the recording of deeds and other papers in Lafayette county.

An act for the relief of soldiers' families.

An act to define the duties of the Trustees of the Internal Improvement Board.

An act making appropriations for the expenses of the first session of the thirteenth General Assembly and for other purposes.

RESOLUTIONS.

Resolution making valid the Election held in Duval County on the first Monday in October, 1864.

Joint Resolution of confidence in and thanks to President Jefferson Davis.

Resolution of thanks to Captain J. J. Dickison.

Resolution for the destruction of redeemed State Treasury Notes and Bonds of 1856 and 1861.

Resolution relative to relief for Soldiers' Families.

Resolution relative to the examination of the offices of Comptroller, Treasurer and Register of Public Lands.

Joint Resolution requesting our Senators and Representatives in Congress to use their influence in procuring the re-enactment of a certain act of Congress

Resolution in relation to the rights of the States.

Resolution of thanks to our Soldiers.

Joint Resolution of thanks to the citizen soldiery of Florida.

Joint Resolution relating to the appointment of an agent at Columbus, Ga.

Resolution in relation to mails in this State.

Resolution in relation to destruction of redeemed Bonds of 1856 and '61 in Treasury office.

Resolution to relieve Archibald C. Black, Tax-Assessor and Collector for Gadsden County.

Resolution for the relief of the Tax-Assessors of Leon and Madison Counties.

Joint Resolution authorizing and requiring the Attorney General to print a general index of the decisions of the Supreme Court, and for other purposes.

Joint Resolution relative to the examination of the Treasurer's and Comptroller's office.

Resolution in relation to estates of deceased persons, orphans and minor children, and their protection from frauds.

Resolution to ask that the Florida brigade in Virginia [be] sent to Department of South Carolina, Georgia and Florida.

Resolution on Confederate relations.

Resolution for the relief of Wm. H. Durrance, W. S. Spencer and Jas. J. Ward

Resolution in relation to the Florida brigade, commanded by Brig. Gen. Finley.

LAWS OF THE STATE OF FLORIDA,

PASSED AT THE

First Session of the Thirteenth General Assembly,

1864.

JOHN MILTON, Governor; B. F. ALLEN, Secretary of State; WALTER GWYNN, Comptroller of Public Accounts; C. H. AUSTIN, Treasurer; J. B. GALBRAITH, Attorney General; A. K. ALLISON, President of the Senate; F. L. VILLEPIGUE, Secretary of the Senate; PHILLIP DELL, Speaker of the House; WM. FORSYTH BYNUM, Clerk of the House.

CHAPTER 1,430—[No. 1.]

AN ACT to create special tribunals for the trial of Capital Offences committed by Slaves, Free Negroes and Mulattoes.

SECTION 1. *Be it enacted by the Senate and House of Representatives of the State of Florida in General Assembly convened*, That slaves, free negroes and mulattoes accused of capital crimes shall be tried by a tribunal composed of two Justices of the Peace and twelve citizens, qualified Jurors of the county where the crime may have been committed. Tribunal composed of two Justices of the Peace.

SEC. 2. *Be it further enacted*, That whenever a slave, free negro or mulatto shall be accused of a capital offence by any person under oath, the Justice of the Peace before whom the complaint is made shall cause the accused to be arrested and confined in the county jail to await his trial, and shall notify another Justice in the county of the charges that have been preferred against such slave, free negro or mulatto, and shall require such Justice to attend at his office the day after the receipt of such notification, or as soon afterwards as practicable, for the purpose of choosing twelve persons, qualified Jurors of the county, to assist at the trial of the accused. Arrest of accused. Notification and attendance of Justices.

SEC. 3. *Be it further enacted*, That the Justices shall select twelve persons, qualified Jurors as aforesaid, who shall be summoned to assemble at the county site of the county, Jurors.

1864.

on a day not exceeding the fifth from the date of the summons, for the purpose of forming the tribunal designated in the two preceding sections, which said summons shall be served by the Sheriff, the Coroner, or any Constable of the county in which the trial is to take place, and the attendance of the Jurors shall be enforced in the same manner as that of other Jurors. In case a sufficient number of Jurors should not appear on the day fixed for trial, then the Justices shall have power to complete the panel by summoning forthwith, from the vicinity, the requisite number of qualified Jurors.

Oath of Jurors.

SEC. 4. *Be it further enacted*, That the Jurors shall be severally sworn truly and impartially to inquire concerning the guilt or innocence of the prisoner or prisoners brought before them, and a true verdict to give according to law and the evidence, to the best of their knowledge, ability and belief.

Justices to take no part in the delineation of the Jury.

SEC. 5. *Be it further enacted*, That the Justices who shall preside at any trial under this act shall take no part in the deliberations of the Jury; but the Jury shall retire and consider of their verdict as in trials before the Circuit Courts of the State. In order to convict the accused, the Jury must unanimously concur in a verdict, to be by them signed, on which verdict the Justices shall endorse the sentence.

Verdict.

Duty of Solicitor.

Clerk of Circuit Court.

SEC. 6. *Be it further enacted*, That it shall be the duty of the Solicitor of the Circuit, when present, to prosecute on behalf of the State, and, in default of such attendance, it shall be lawful for the Justices to appoint some attorney to act as prosecutor. The Clerk of the Circuit Court of the county in which the trial shall take place shall act as clerk of the special tribunal, and keep full minutes of the proceedings thereof.

Appeals.

SEC. 7. *Be it further enacted*, That appeals from the judgment of such tribunals shall be had to the Circuit Court of the county upon an order made by the Judge thereof upon an inspection of the record of the trial, and such appeal, when allowed, shall operate as a *supersedeas* of the judgment; but no proceedings shall be annulled or impeded by any error of form.

Sentence.

Execution.

Umpire.

SEC. 8. *Be it further enacted*, That in case the offender shall be convicted of a capital offence, the Justices shall sign a sentence of death by hanging, which shall be executed by the Sheriff of the county at such time and place as the Justies may appoint; and in case said Justices cannot agree, they shall call in a third Justice as umpire to decide.

Passed the Senate November 25, 1864. Passed the House of Representatives November 29, 1864. Approved by the Governor December 2, 1864.

CHAPTER 1,431—[No. 2.]

AN ACT to amend an act entitled an act to establish and permanently locate the county site of Manatee county, approved December 5th, 1861.

SECTION 1. *Be it enacted by the Senate and House of Representatives of the State of Florida in General Assembly convened,* That an act entitled "An act to establish and permanently locate the county site of Manatee county" be so amended that all Courts and public offices required by law to be held at the county site shall continue to be held at the former Court House, in the town of Manatee, until such time as a suitable house shall be provided for that purpose at the new county site.

Courts and public offices to be held at the town of Manatee.

Passed the House of Representatives November 30, 1864. Passed the Senate December 1, 1864. Approved by the Governor December 3d, 1864.

CHAPTER 1,432.—[No. 3.]

AN ACT to repeal an act entitled "An Act to consolidate the offices of Clerk of the Circuit Court and Judge of Probate in and for Manatee county," approved December 8, 1862.

SECTION 1. *Be it enacted by the Senate and House of Representatives of the State of Florida in General Assembly convened,* That an act entitled "An act to consolidate the offices of the Clerk of the Circuit Court and Judge of Probate of Manatee county," approved December 8, 1862, be and the same is hereby repealed, said repeal to take effect from and after the first Monday in October, 1865.

Repeal.

SEC. 2. *Be it further enacted,* That an election for a Clerk of the Circuit Court of Manatee county be henceforth held at the regular time of election, as directed by law for other counties of the State of Florida.

Election for Clerk of Circuit Court.

Passed the House of Representatives November 30th, 1864. Passed the Senate December 1st, 1864. Approved by the Governor December 3d, 1864.

CHAPTER 1,433—[No. 4.]

AN ACT to organize Militia Troops for the State of Florida.

Persons subject to militia duty.

SECTION 1. *Be it enacted by the Senate and House of Representatives of the State of Florida, in General Assembly convened*, That every able-bodied white male inhabitant in this State, between the ages of sixteen and fifty-five years, not included in the Military service of the Confederate States, and who is physically able to perform Militia duty, whether citizen, resident or sojourner, with the exceptions hereinafter specified, is hereby declared to be in the Militia service of the State of Florida, and shall be immediately enrolled and liable to perform Militia duty in the Militia forces that now are or may hereafter be organized, and no person shall be exempt for physical incapacity unless in the manner hereinafter provided.

Organization to be preserved.

SEC. 2. *Be it further enacted*, That each and every company, regiment or battalion organized in pursuance of General Orders No. 11, dated July 30th, 1864, issued by the Governor and Commander-in-Chief, shall continue in their present organization, and the commissions of their officers shall continue in full force and virtue: *Provided, nevertheless*, That should a majority of the enrolled members of any company, regiment or battalion, organized in pursuance of said General Orders No. 11, represent by petition to the Commander-in-Chief, within twenty days from the passage of this act, that a change of officers would promote the efficiency of said company, regiment or battalion; then, and in that case, the Governor shall declare the commissions of the present officers vacated, and a new election for officers thereof shall be ordered within ten days thereafter, in case of a company, and twenty days in case of a regiment or battalion; and every person liable to Militiaduty, under this act, shall enroll himself in some company in his county within ten days from the proclamation of the Governor, under this act, unless said company exceed the number of sixty-four men, in which case they may form another company of not less than thirty-five men; in which case they may elect one Captain, one First Lieutenant and two Second Lieutenants; and if any person shall fail or refuse to enroll himself, he shall be fined or imprisoned at the discretion of a General Court Martial: *Provided*, That in counties where no company is now organized, the persons liable to Militia duty therein

Proviso as to change of officers.

New election.

Persons liable to militia duty must enrol themselves.

Other companies may be formed.

Officers.

Persons failing to enrol themselves.

In counties where no organization.

shall be forthwith organized by the Adjutant and Inspector General, under such rules and regulations as he may prescribe, not inconsistent with the provisions of this act: *Provided, further,* That all companies hereafter to be organized under this act, shall elect their respective commissioned officers. *And provided, further,* That should such persons as are embraced in this provision fail to organize themselves in such time as the Adjutant and Inspector General shall prescribe, they shall be liable to the pains and penalties imposed by this act.

Election o cers.

Persons f to organiz

SEC. 3. *Be it further enacted,* That the Governor shall prescribe such rules and regulations as may be necessary to insure an efficient organization of the Militia forces organized or hereafter to be organized by this act, and to promote their effectiveness; and for that purpose he may organize the said Militia into such new battalions, regiments, brigade or brigades, as the defence of the State may require: *Provided, however,* That the commissioned officers shall be elected by the men of their commands.

Govern prescribe and regu

Battalion iments,

SEC. 4. *Be it further enacted,* That the Militia, when in service in the field for the defence of the State, shall be subject to the rules and articles of war of the Confederate States, and any officer or other person failing to perform or refusing to discharge the militia duty enjoined upon him by this act, or refusing to obey any legal order of any superior officer, or of the Governor (and) Commander-in-Chief, or of any superior officer, shall be punished at the discretion of a General Court Martial: *Provided, however,* Each company may adopt by-laws for their own government not inconsistent with the provisions of this act, when not in service under orders of the Governor; and said by-laws shall be enforced by company Court Martial: *Provided,* That the findings of said company Court Martial shall be first approved by the Governor; and if any commissioned officer shall be guilty of drunkenness while on duty, or of general intemperance, whether on duty or not, or of conduct unbecoming an officer and a gentleman, or of disobedience of orders, or of incompetency, he shall be deprived of his commission by sentence of a General Court Martial. All General Court Martials shall be ordered by the Governor, and consist of not less than five nor more than thirteen commissioned officers.

Militi in the f ject to cles of

Punish disobed

Com laws.

Court

Inte &c.

Ger Marti

SEC. 5. *Be it further enacted,* That, at each militia drill, the Captains of each company shall have detailed from their commands a sufficient number of men to keep up a vigilant

Pa

1864. patrol within each militia beat, which patrol is to be performed until the next drill.

and equip
SEC. 6. *Be it further enacted*, That the Governor shall cause the militia to be armed and equipped as expeditiously as possible.

rnor may militia to to Con. for de- of the
SEC. 7. *Be it further enacted*, That whenever the Confederate officer commanding in this State shall call upon the Governor for troops to defend the State, the Governor is hereby authorized to order any portion of the Militia to report to the officer commanding the Confederate forces; and that whenever any Confederate officer in this State shall call upon the Governor, and, if impossible to do so, shall call upon any officer commanding any of the Militia of this State for aid in repulsing the enemy, it shall be his or their duty to render all the aid in their power; and the Governor shall require the return of the Militia as soon as the emergency for which they have been called shall, in his opinion, no longer require their services.

n of mi-

c of in- ion.
SEC. 8. *Be it further enacted*, That in cases of survile insurrection or actual raids of the enemy, the Governor shall have the power, and it shall be his duty to call the Militia into active service for the purpose of suppressing such insurrection or repelling such actual raids; and the Militia shall not remain in active service any longer than shall be necessary to quell the insurrection or repel the raid: *Provided*, That in no instance and under no circumstances shall those persons of the Militia who shall be over fifty years of age be required or compelled to march beyond the limits of the Military District in which they may reside; and if not incompatible with the public service the Governor shall cause and require said persons to remain in their respective counties.

is over of age be or- eyond trict.

Court
SEC. 9. *Be it further enacted*, That Company Court Martials shall consist of one commissioned officer, one non-commissioned officer and three privates of the Company, and the sentences of said Court Martial shall be carried into execution by the Sheriff of the county; *Provided, however*, No Company Court Martial shall punish except by fine not exceeding One Hundred Dollars, or by imprisonment not exceeding ten days; and where fines are imposed they shall be collected by the Sheriff, by levy and sale, and shall be payable in the currency of the country, which Court Martial shall be appointed by the Captain of the Company.

ions.
SEC. 10. *Be it further enacted*, That no person enbraced within the ages of 16 and 55 years aforesaid, shall be exempt

from Militia duty, except the following: 1st, Every person who is or may become physically unable to perform Militia duty, to be ascertained in such manner as the Governor shall prescribe; 2d, ministers of religion who now are in the regular discharge of their ministerial duties; 3d, Judges of the Supreme and Circuit Courts; 4th, millers, not exceeding one for each mill; 5th, ferrymen on post routes; 6th, physicians of 40 years of age; 7th, members and officers of the Legislature when in actual session: *Provided*, That nothing herein shall be so construed as to deprive the members and officers of the Legislature from attending any regular or extra session of the Legislature without delay, let or hindrance.

Militia districts

SEC. 11. *Be it further enacted*, That this State is hereby divided into three Militia districts. The first district shall comprise all that part of the State that lies east of the Suwannee river; the second district all that part lying between the Suwannee and Apalachicola river, and the third district all that part lying west of the Apalachicola river.

Repeal.

SEC. 12. *Be it further enacted* That all laws and parts of laws inconsistent with this act be and they are hereby repealed.

Passed the Senate November 30, 1864. Passed the House of Representatives December 2, 1864. Approved December 5, 1864.

CHAPTER 1,434—[No. 5.]

AN ACT to amend the laws relating to Slaves.

Duty of Sheriffs in relation to slaves hiring their own time.

SECTION 1. *Be it enacted by the Senate and House of Representatives of the State of Florida in General Assembly convened*, That it shall be the duty of the Sheriffs of the several counties in this State to ascertain and inform against all persons, and to arrest and commit to jail all slaves, who shall violate the laws of this State made and provided against slaves hiring their own time.

Sheriff neglecting duty, fined.

SEC. 2. *Be it further enacted*, That if any Sheriff shall wilfully refuse or fail to discharge the duties as imposed by this act, he shall, on conviction thereof, be fined in a sum not less than five hundred, nor more than one thousand dollars.

Passed the Senate November 26, 1864. Passed the House of Representatives December 1, 1864. Approved by the Governor December 5, 1864.

Chapter 1,435—[No. 6.]

AN ACT relating to the accounts of Ex-Governor M. S. Perry and H. V. Snell, late Quartermaster General.

Preamble.

Whereas, The unsettled accounts of Ex-Governor M. S. Perry and of H. V. Snell, late Quarter-Master General, have been examined by Samuel Benezet, Esq., Accountant; appointed under a joint resolution of the General Assembly, and whereas said Accountant has reported to this General Assembly the accounts of said parties adjusted by him; and whereas, there is due to said Ex-Governor M. S. Perry the sum of six thousand five hundred and sixty-seven dollars and nine cents, and to said H. V. Snell, late Quarter-Master General, the sum of ten thousand two hundred dollars and thirty-five cents; and, whereas, by the joint resolution under which said Accountant was appointed, it is provided "that the expenses of said Accountant shall be equally divided between the State of Florida and each of said persons —Therefore,

Comptroller to issue warrant in favor Ex Gov. M. S. Perry & others.

Secton 1. *Be it enacted by the Senate and House of Representatives of the State of Florida in General Assembly convened*, That the Comptroller is hereby ordered to issue his warrant upon the Treasurer in favor of Ex-Governor M. S. Perry for the sum of five thousand five hundred and sixty-seven dollars and nine cents, and in favor of S. Benezet, Accountant, for the sum of one thousand dollars, the same being in full of the amount due said Ex-Governor M. S. Perry, and the Comptroller is hereby ordered to issue his warrant upon the Treasurer in favor of H. V. Snell, late Quatrer-Master General, for the sum of nine thousand two hundred dollars and thirty-five cents, and in favor of S. Benezet, Accountant, for the sum of one thousand dollars, the same being in full of the amount due said H. V. Snell, late Quartermaster General.

Comptroller to issue warrant, &c.

Sec. 2. *Be it further enacted*, That the Comptroller be and he is hereby ordered to issue his warrant upon the Treasurer in favor of S. Benezet, Accountant, for the sum of one thousand dollars, the same being in full of the amount due by the State to said Accountant.

Passed the House of Representatives November 26th, 1864. Passed the Senate December 1, 1864. Approved by the Governor December 5th, 1864.

CHAPTER 1,436—[No. 7.]

AN ACT relating to holding Commissioner's Courts of Lafayette County.

SECTION 1. *Be it enacted by the Senate and House of Representatives of the State of Florida in General Assembly convened,* That the County Commissioners of Lafayette County be authorized to hold the Commissioners' Courts of said County at Moseley's Mills, or at any other place in said County, or in an adjacent County, which may be the most convenient and safe as said Commissioners may determine, upon giving public notice, by posting in the public places in said County, or in some newspaper in this State; and that all Courts heretofore held by said Commissioners at Moseley's Mills in said County shall be as valid in law as if held in the County site of said County: *Provided, however,* That this act shall be in force and effect until such time as said County Commissioners shall deem it safe to resume the holding of said Commissioners' Courts at the County site of said County. Com's Courts where held. Limitation.

SEC. 2. *Be it further enacted,* That all laws and parts of laws conflicting against this Act be and the same are hereby repealed. Repeal.

Passed the House of Representatives November 30, 1864. Passed the Senate December 2, 1864. Approved by the Governor December 5th, 1864.

CHAPTER 1,437—[No. 8.]

AN ACT to amend an act entitled "An Act for the protection of Cattle owners in the counties of Levy, Lafayette, Taylor, Wakulla and Duval," approved November 27, 1863.

SECTION 1. *Be it enacted by the Senate and House of Representatives of the State of Florida in General Assembly convened,* That the above entitled act be so amended, that the prohibitions and penalties therein contained shall, after the passage of this act, be imperative and inapplicable from the first day of April to the first day of September of each year, and that all acts and parts of acts contrary to, or conflicting with this act, be and they are hereby repealed. Limitation of Act. Repeal.

SEC. 2. *Be it further enacted,* That the provisions of the act to which this is an amendment, as amended by this act, be Provisions of amendment extended to other counties.

1864. extended to include the counties of Brevard, Hernando, Orange and Sumter, to the same extent that would have been if they had been specially named in said original act.

Passed the House of Representatives November 30, 1864. Passed the Senate December 3, 1864. Approved by the Governor December 5, 1864.

CHAPTER 1,438—[No. 9.]

AN ACT for the relief of our sick and wounded Soldiers.

SECTION 1. *Be it enacted by the Senate and House of Representatives of the State of Florida in General Assembly convened*, That there be and is hereby appropriated the sum of sixty thousand dollars, for the purpose of aiding the sick and wounded soldiers from this State, which sum shall be expended from time to time as the Governor may direct, and in such manner as he may prescribe, and the Governor shall for that purpose issue his orders upon the Comptroller, who shall draw a warrant on the Treasurer for the amount specified on the order of the Governor, and the Treasurer shall pay the same.

Appropriation.

Governor to direct expenditure.

Passed the House of Representatives November 30, 1864. Passed the Senate December 1, 1864. Approved by the Governor December 5, 1864.

CHAPTER 1,439—[No. 10.]

AN ACT to provide for the appointment of County Officers in certain cases.

SECTION 1. *Be it enacted by the Senate and House of Representatives of the State of Florida in General Assembly convened*, That if at any time any Sheriff, Circuit Clerk, Tax-Assessor or Collector, Coroner, County Surveyor, Judge of Probate or County Commissioner shall be taken prisoner by the public enemy, so that he cannot perform the duties of his office, it shall be lawful for the Governor, and he is hereby authorized and required to appoint, a fit and proper person in the place of the officer so taken prisoner, who shall hold and discharge the duties of said officer until the officer is released from captivity and returns to the county from

Officers that may be appointed and in what cases.

Gov'nor shall make appointment.

which he was taken, or the term of office of said person expires by legal limitation.

SEC. 2. *Be it further enacted*, That whenever the Governor shall appoint an officer under the first section of this act, it shall be lawful for him to require of the officer, so appointed, like bond and security, conditioned for the faithful discharge of his official duties, as was required of the officer taken prisoner by the enemy: *Provided, however*, This act shall not be construed to deprive or take away the power vested by law in any Judge of a Circuit Court when a vacancy occurs in the office of Clerk or Sheriff, if the said Judge is in the discharge of his duties.

Bond of officer.

Proviso.

SEC. 3. *Be it further enacted*, That whenever any of the officers mentioned in the first section are in the service of the Confederate States, so that they cannot perform the duties of their office, the Governor shall have the power to appoint, as is provided in said first section, which appointment shall continue until the discharge of the officer from said service or the term of office expires by legal limitation.

Officers in service of Confed. States.

SEC. 4. *And be it further enacted*, That the Governor be requested to appoint such county officers as were duly elected by the people, on the first Monday in October, 1864.

County officers elected in Oct, 1864.

Passed the House of Representatives November 26, 1864. Passed the Senate December 2, 1864. Approved by the Governor December 5, 1864.

CHAPTER 1,440—[No. 11.]

AN ACT to authorize William F. Russell to enter one hundred and sixty acres of Land.

WHEREAS, William F. Russell did enter one hundred and sixty acres of land in Marion county, which land has since been sold by the State of Florida since the Ordinance of Secession—Therefore,

Preamble.

SECTION 1. *Be it enacted by the Senate and House of Representatives of the State of Florida in General Assembly convened*, That William F. Russell be and he is hereby authorized to enter, free of charge, one hundred and sixty acres of the Public Lands of Florida, liable to entry, and which are not by law selected for School or Seminary, or Internal Improvement Lands, and the Receiver is hereby authorized to issue a patent therefor as in cases of sale.

Resolution.

Passed the Senate December 3, 1864. Passed the House of Representatives December 5, 1864. Approved by the Governor December 6, 1864.

1864.

CHAPTER 1,441—[No. 12.]

AN ACT to provide for taking the Census in the year 1865 in this State.

Tax Assessors made census takers.

SECTION 1. *Be it enacted by the Senate and House of Representatives of the State of Florida in General Assembly convened,* That the Tax-Assessors and Collectors of the several counties in this State be and they are hereby constituted and appointed takers of the census of the inhabitants of their respective counties for the year eighteen hundred and sixty-five.

Enumeration of inhabitants.

List.

SEC. 2. *Be it further enacted,* That the said Tax-Assessors and Collectors shall proceed to make an enumeration of all the inhabitants of their respective counties, distinguishing the free white inhabitants, slaves and free persons of color therein residing, and making a list, or statement in duplicate, accurately prepared, of such inhabitants and such enumeration, one copy of which list shall be filed in the office of the Judge of Probate of the respective counties, and the other returned to the Secretary of State.

Returns.

Compensation.

SEC. 2 *Be it further enacted,* That the said enumeration shall be made and the return thereof made to the Secretary of State by said takers of the census on or before the first day of September, A. D. 1865; and as compensation for their services under this act, the said census takers shall receive ten cents per capita for the first thousand inhabitants, and six cents for all over one thousand and under three thousand, and four cents for all over three thousand; and for all counties having less than five hundred inhabitants, sixteen cents for each inhabitant, which amount shall be paid in each case by warrant of the Comptroller upon certificate of the Secretary of State that the duties required of the said takers of the census have been discharged properly and the return made to his office according to law.

Appropriation.

Forms.

SEC. 4. *Be it further enacted,* That for the purpose of carrying out the provisions of this act, the sum of ten thousand dollars is hereby appropriated out of any money in the Treasury not otherwise appropriated; and that the Secretary of State shall, under the direction of the Governor, furnish suitable printed forms to the census takers herein provided for, which forms shall give such directions as to the particulars of the enumeration herein provided for as may by the Governor be deemed proper and expedient, and which forms and directions shall in all respects be accurately observed by said census takers in making said enumeration.

Tax Assessor failing to do duty.

SEC. 5. *Be it further enacted,* That if any Tax-Assessor shall fail, refuse or neglect to perform any of the duties imposed by this act, he shall be guilty of a misdemeanor, and shall be subject to a fine of not less than one thousand dollars at the discretion of court.

Passed the House of Representatives December 1, 1864. Passed the Senate December 2, 1864. Approved by the Governor December 6, 1864.

CHAPTER 1,442—[No. 13.]

AN ACT to amend "An Act to provide for the establishment of two Seminaries of Learning.

SECTION 1. *Be it enacted by the Senate and House of Representatives of the State of Florida in General Assembly convened,* That that portion of the 3d Section of an "Act to provide for the establishment of two Seminaries of Learning," approved January 24, 1851, which provides that the County Superintendent of the county in which such Seminaries are situated shall be ex-officio a member and Secretary of the Board of Education for each Seminary, be and the same is hereby so amended as to relieve the Judge of Probate or County Superintendent of Leon county from the discharge of said functions and duties: *Provided,* That the Governor shall appoint some suitable person to fill the place of member of the Board of Education for the Seminary West of the Suwannee, made vacant by the provisions of this act.

County superintendant.

Governor to appoint.

Passed the House of Representatives December 3, 1864. Passed the Senate December 5, 1864. Approved by the Governor December 6, 1864.

CHAPTER 1,443—[No. 14.]

AN ACT for the Education of Soldiers' Children.

SECTION 1. *Be it enacted by the Senate and House of Representatives of the State of Florida in General Assembly convened,* That it shall be the duty of the Board of County Commissioners of each county in this State to have a list made of all the orphan children of every deceased soldier or sailor who, when he enlisted in the service of the State of Florida or of the Confederate States, resided in the State of Florida, and of all children of soldiers or sailors who now are or have been in either of said services and whose circumstances are such as to prevent such parent from giving his child or children a suitable education; and upon said list being perfected, a copy shall be sent to the Governor, and it shall be the duty of said County Commissioners to send each and every child herein provided for to some suitable school nearest the residence of the child, and, where there is no such school, to establish such number as may be necessary to insure an English education to all such children in their respective counties, and to provide male or female teachers therefor; and they shall examine and certify to the several accounts which exhibit the sums of money which are actually necessary for the purposes aforesaid, and send the same to the Governor for his

List of children of soldiers.

County Commissioners to send children to school.

Teachers.

Accounts.

1864.

examination, who, if he shall approve the same, shall issue his order thereon for payment, but if he shall disapprove of the same, it shall be sent back to the County Commissioners for correction; and the Comptroller shall draw his warrant on the order of the Governor and the Treasurer shall pay the same. And whenever by any cause whatever the County Commissoners of any county shall fail or be unable to perform the duties herein enjoined upon them, or whenever by reason of any cause there is no Board of County Commissioners, the Governor shall appoint a suitable person for such county, who shall discharge the duties herein enjoined upon the County Commissioners.

Warrant for payment.

County Commissioners failing to perform duty.

Sec. 2. *Be it further enacted,* That all such schools and teachers shall be under the especial control and guardianship of the Governor, who shall from time to time require the same to be visited by suitable persons to be appointed by him, and report to be made to him, and he shall make and prescribe such rules and regulations as to insure to each child in this act provided for an English education.

Governor to control and direct schools.

Sec. 3. *Be it further enacted,* That there shall be levied and collected a tax upon all property now by law taxed by the general tax laws of this State, and in the same manner and at the same time and places a tax of one-third of one-sixth of one per cent., which shall form a special fund for the purposes of this act.

Tax.

Passed the House of Representatives November 30, 1864. Passed the Senate December 1, 1864. Approved by the Governor December 6, 1864.

Note.—The words "of one" have been inserted in the text of the above act, so that the section will read "one-third of one-sixth of one per cent." Although in the enrolled act the words "of one" are omitted, as well as in the engrossed bill, which has been examined, yet the original bill contains these words, which have probably been omitted in the engrossed and enrolled bills by oversight or mistake, as it is not probable that the General Assembly could have intended to impose such a tax as that provided by the act as enrolled for the purposes contemplated therein.

Chapter 1,444—[No. 15.]

AN ACT to amend an act entitled "An Act to allow the Supreme Court of this State to hold extra terms in certain cases therein specified," approved December 28, 1864.

Section 1. *Be it enacted by the Senate and House of Representatives of the State of Florida in General Assembly convened,* That hereafter it shall and may be lawful for the respective Judges of the Circuit Courts of this State to hold extra or adjourned terms of said Courts, whenever said Courts shall not

Circuit Judges may hold extra and adjourned terms.

have been holden at the time or times prescribed by law in consequence of the presence of the enemy or for any other causes, and it shall be the duty of the Judges, in such cases, to appoint a convenient day or days for the holding of such extra or adjourned terms whenever there shall have been a failure from any cause of the regular terms.

Governor may appoint or assign other Judge in case of absence of incumbent.

SEC. 2. *Be it further enacted*, That whenever it shall appear to the Governor of this State, that any Judge of the Circuit Court in either of the Judicial Circuits of this State is absent from his Circuit and cannot hold the Courts of the same, it shall be lawful for the Governor, and he is hereby authorized and required, to appoint and assign one of the Judges of the Circuit Court to hold the terms of the Court in the Circuit at such time or times as the Governor may direct.

Judge failing to perform duty

SEC. 3. *Be it further enacted*, That if any Judge shall fail in the performance of the duty required of him by the Governor, under the preceding section of this act, such failure shall be cause of impeachment of such Judge.

Compensation.

SEC. 4. *Be it further enacted*, That the Judges of the Circuit Court shall receive an increased compensation sufficient to reimburse them for the increased expense to which they may be subject in performing the duties required by this act, to be paid on the warrant of the Comptroller to be issued upon the certificate of the Governor.

Judicial business of Western Circuit.

SEC. 5. *Be it further enacted*, That whenever there is any legal business which could have been determined in the Western Circuit at Chambers, the same may be heard and determined before the Judge of the Middle Circuit at his Chamber, upon giving notice thereof to the opposite party, plaintiff or defendant, during the absence of the Judge of the Western Circuit.

Passed the House of Representatives November 26, 1864. Passed the Senate December 1, 1864. Approved by the Governor December 6, 1864.

CHAPTER 1,445—[No. 16.]

AN ACT to fix the County Site of Brevard County, and for other purposes.

County site.

SECTION 1. *Be it enacted by the Senate and House of Representatives of the State of Florida in General Assembly convened*, That the county site of Brevard county shall be and the same is hereby located at Bassville, in said county, and that all records and county offices shall be held and kept at said county site.

Election of county officers.

SEC. 2. *Be it further enacted*, That there shall be an election held in said county on the first Monday in March next, to fill any

1864.

vacancies that may exist in the county offices of said county, and that from and after the passage of this act, all the county business of said county shall be done and transacted in said county of Brevard, by its own county officers, in like manner as in other counties of this State, and any election heretofore held for such officers are hereby legalized and made valid.

Repeal.

SEC. 3. *Be it further enacted*, That all laws and parts of laws conflicting with the provisions of this act be and the same are hereby repealed.

Passed the House of Representatives November 30, 1864. Passed the Senate December 5, 1864. Approved by the Governor December 6, 1864.

CHAPTER 1,446—[No. 17.]

AN ACT to facilitate the transaction of business in the Quartermaster General's Office.

Quartermaster to make estimate of expenditures.

Comptroller to issue warrant.

SECTION 1. *Be it enacted by the Senate and House of Representatives of the State of Florida in General Assembly convened*, That the Quartermaster General shall make quarterly estimates of the amount of money required for the ensuing quarter for the use of his department, which estimate shall be exhibited to the Governor, and if the Governor approve such estimate, he shall draw an order on the Comptroller for the amount, and the Comptroller shall issue a warrant thereon in favor of the Quartermaster General, and the Treasurer shall pay the same.

Quartermasters accounts.

Proviso.

SEC. 2. *Be it further enacted*, That at the expiration of each quarter, the Quartermaster General shall present his accounts and vouchers to the Comptroller, who shall audit and allow all payments made according to law: *Provided, however*, The amount appropriated shall not exceed three thousand dollars to meet the quarterly estimates of the Quartermaster.

Passed the Senate November 28, 1864. Passed the House of Representatives December 3, 1864. Approved by the Governor December 6, 1864.

CHAPTER 1,447—[No. 18.]

AN ACT in relation to Estates in this State.

Estates may be kept together.

SECTION 1. *Be it enacted by the Senate and House of Representatives of the State of Florida in General Assembly convened*, That whenever, in the opinion of the administrator or executor, or any person having any interest in any estate, real or personal, in this State, it would be detrimental to have such estate sold or hired or rented during the war, such person or persons may file a petition, under oath, before the Judge of Probate of the county where the estate is situated, setting forth the facts and praying for an order to have said estate kept together and carried on, or to have said estate divided among the heirs or distributees.

Commissioners in regard to management of estate.

SEC. 2. *Be it further enacted*, That upon the filing of said petition, it shall be the duty of the Judge of Probate to appoint three suitable disinterested persons, citizens of the county, as Commissioners, who shall report upon oath whether it is advisable to sell the personal property and slaves, or to sell a part and hire a part or portion of such slaves or personal property, or to hire or rent the whole of the lands, slaves, or personal property comprising the estate, or to have said estate kept together and the same engaged in planting or the usual business that said estate was employed in; and the Judge of Probate shall issue his order in conformity to the report of the Commissioners: *Provided, however*, The adminisinstrator or executor, or any other person interested in said estate, may take an appeal to the Judge of the Circuit Court from said order, upon giving notice in writing to the administrator or executor of said estate, which appeal may be taken at the time; and the Judge of the Circuit Court shall hear the whole matter *de novo*, and shall issue such order as he may deem necessary to arrive at a final judgment.

Appeal.

Petition of estate.

SEC. 3. *Be it further enacted*, That nothing in this act shall be so construed as to prevent partition of real or personal property, as now by law provided.

Confederate funds.

SEC. 4. *Be it further enacted*, That administrators and executors and guardians who may have received Confederate money, or who may have invested funds of estates in their hands in Confederate bonds, shall be permitted to sell the same and reinvest the proceeds thereof in six per cent. non-taxable bonds of the Confederate States.

Widow entitled to wearing apparel, &c., separate from dower.

SEC. 5. *Be it further enacted*, That when any person dying intestate shall leave a widow, she shall be entitled to keep her wearing apparel and such household goods and farming utensils, provisions and clothing, as may be necessary for her maintenance and that of her family, to be set apart by the appraisers, who shall have special regard to the ability of such widow and children to provide for and maintain themselves; and the aforesaid articles shall not be considered and taken as forming a part of the widow's dower in any case.

Repeal.

SEC. 6. *Be it further enacted*, That all laws and parts of laws conflicting with this act be and they are hereby repealed.

Passed the Senate November 26, 1864. Passed the House of Representatives December 5, 1864. Approved by the Governor December 6, 1864.

CHAPTER 1,448—[No. 19.]

AN ACT to increase the price of Public Lands.

SECTION 1. *Be it enacted by the Senate and House of Representatives of the State of Florida in General Assembly convened,*

Price of lands.

That, from and after the first day of January next, the price of the public lands of this State, acquired by secession, shall be ten dollars per acre for hammock lands, and five dollars per acre for other lands; and the purchaser shall pay in addition thereto the sum of five per cent. upon the amount of purchase money as commissions to the Register or Receiver, and such Register or Receiver shall not charge the State for commissions upon entries hereafter made, except entries made by soldiers or their widows, or minor children.

Commissions.

Price of School and Seminary lands.

SEC. 2. *Be it further enacted,* That the price of the School and Seminary lands be and they are hereby increased to five times the price at which they are now held.

Passed the Senate December 3, 1864. Passed the House of Representatives December 5, 1864. Approved by the Governor December 7, 1864.

CHAPTER 1,449—[No. 20.]

AN ACT to amend the laws providing for the Stay of Executions.

SECTION 1. *Be it enacted by the Senate and House of Representatives of the State of Florida in General Assembly convened,*

Soldiers in Confed. service.

That, from and after the passage of this act, it shall not be lawful to demand from any soldier who now is or has been in the service of the Confederate States, and who may have been honorably discharged from the same, the bond required to be given by the first section of an "Act providing for the Stay of Executions in this State," approved December 13, 1861.

Passed the House of Representatives November 30, 1864. Passed the Senate December 7, 1864. Approved by the Governor December 7, 1864.

CHAPTER 1,450—[No. 21.]

AN ACT to amend "An Act to incorporate the City of Lake City."

SECTION. 1. *Be it enacted by the Senate and House of Representatives of the State of Florida in General Assembly convened,*

Corporate limits.

That the corporate limits of the city of Lake City be and they are hereby declared to be comprehended within the following bounds, that is to say, three-quarters of a mile north, south, east and west of the Court House of Columbia county, in every direction therefrom.

SEC. 2. *Be it further enacted*, That the City Council of Lake City be and they are hereby authorized and empowered to appoint a city Surveyor, a city Physician and city Attorneys, if in their judgment they shall deem such officers and appointments necessary or proper to be made. City Surveyor.

Passed the House of Representatives December 3, 1864. Passed the Senate December 6, 1864. Approved by the Governor December 7, 1864.

CHAPTER 1,451—[No. 22.]

AN ACT to authorize the Administrator of the estate of Anna L. Casey to make title to certain lots in Columbia County.

WHEREAS, Anna L. Casey, late of the county of Columbia, did, previous to her decease, give to the Catholic Church of the city of Lake City, in said county, a certain lot of land in said place for Church purposes, and declared her intention to perfect titles to the same, but was prevented by death from so doing; and, whereas, the said decedent died intestate and without heirs or devisees; and, whereas, it is deemed proper that her intention to convey said property shall be allowed to be carried into effect—Therefore, Preamble.

SECTION 1. *Be it enacted by the Senate and House of Representatives of the State of Florida in General Assembly convened*, That the Administrator of the estate of said Anna L. Casey be and he is hereby authorized to carry out the intention of said decedent, and to make such titles to said property as may be deemed necessary and proper [to] effect that purpose. Administrator to make title.

Passed the House of Representatives December 3, 1864. Passed the Senate December 6, 1864. Approved by the Governor December 7, 1864.

CHAPTER 1,452—[No. 23.]

AN ACT in relation to the the commissions of Executors, Guardians, Curators and Administrators.

SECTION 1. *Be it enacted by the Senate and House of Representatives of the State of Florida in General Assembly convened*, That the commissions of executors, guardians, curators Executors, &c., in military service.

1864.

and administrators who are in the military service of the Confederate States be allowed them, whether they make their annual returns within the time prescribed by law or not: *Provided*, That within three months after their discharge from said service, or within three months after the termination of the war, they shall file all returns then due.

Commissions forfeited to be allowed.

SEC. 2. *Be it further enacted*, That all commissions which have heretofore been forfeited by such persons, whether in the Confederate States or State service, be allowed them: *Provided*, They shall file all returns due within the time mentioned in the first section of this act.

Returns may be made by Attorney.

SEC. 3. *Be it further enacted*, That the returns now by law required to be made, may be made by the agent or attorney *de facto* of the persons specified in the first section of this act.

Passed the Senate December 5, 1864. Passed the House of Representatives December 7, 1864. Approved by the Governor December 7, 1864.

CHAPTER 1,453—[No. 24.]

AN ACT to amend an Act entitled "An Act to amend the Election Laws of this State as regards the mode of voting, and for other purposes," approved December 8, 1862.

SECTION 1. *Be it enacted by the Senate and House of Representatives of the State of Florida in General Assembly convened*, That so much of an act entitled "An act to amend the election laws of this State as regards the mode of voting, and for other purposes, "approved Dec. 8, 1862, as requires that the Inspectors of elections shall number the ballots given at any election to correspond with the name of the voter on the poll-book, be and the same is hereby repealed.

Passed the House of Representatives December 2, 1864. Passed the Senate December 6, 1864. Approved by the Governor December 7, 1864.

CHAPTER 1,454—[No. 25.]

AN ACT to appropriate a Fund for clothing of troops from Florida in the Confederate service, and to purchase and distribute Cards.

Appropriation.

SECTION 1. *Be it enacted by the Senate and House of Representatives of the State of Florida in General Assembly convened*, That the sum of fifty thousand dollars, or so much of the same as the Governor may deem necessary, be and it is hereby appropriated and placed at the disposal of the Governor, to provide clothing for troops from Florida in the Confederate service, to be used to meet contingencies and only in case of necessity and for special occasions and circumstances.

Cotton Cards to be purchased.

SEC. 2. *Be it further enacted*, That the Governor be and he is hereby authorized and required to contract for and purchase, at home or abroad, three thousand pairs of cotton cards, for the aid of soldiers' families and others that require assistance, as specified in the "act to provide for the relief of soldiers' families and others that require assistance," approved by the Governor, December 3, 1863, and to cause the same to be distributed among the several counties for distribution to the poor; and the Governor shall issue his order on the Comptroller for the money necessary to purchase cards, and the Comptroller shall issue his warrant for the same, and the Treasurer shall pay the same; and the sum of fifty thousand dollars is hereby appropriated to carry out the purposes of this section.

Distribution.

Appropriation.

Passed the House of Representatives December 5, 1864. Passed the Senate December 6, 1864. Approved by the Governor December 7, 1864.

CHAPTER 1,455—[No. 26.]

AN ACT relative to the fees of the Clerk of the Supreme Court and Jailors.

SECTION 1. *Be it enacted by the Senate and House of Representatives of the State of Florida in General Assembly convened*, That the Clerk of the Supreme Court shall be entitled to demand and receive the same increase of fees as was allowed to the Clerks of the Circuit Courts by "An Act to raise the salary of the State Treasurer and other officers therein named," approved November 30, 1863.

Clerk Supreme Court fees increased.

SEC. 2. *Be it further enacted*, That the Sheriff or Jailors of this State be allowed two dollars per day, fees, for taking care of prisoners, instead of one dollar, which are the fees now allowed by law.

Sheriffs & Jailors fees.

Passed the House of Representatives December 5, 1864. Passed the Senate December 5, 1864. Approved by the Governor December 7, 1864.

CHAPTER 1,456—[No. 27.]

AN ACT in relation to the Public Defence.

SECTION 1. *Be it enacted by the Senate and House of Representatives of the State of Florida in General Assembly convened*, That whenever a demand shall be made by the Confederate States Government for slaves to labor on the public works in

Impressement of slaves for labor on public works.

1864.

this State, and such demand be in conformity with the laws of the Confederate States and with the Constitution and laws of the State of Florida, the Governor of this State shall order an impressment *pro rata*, which shall be strictly uniform and equitable, of the free negroes and slaves in this State.

Sheriffs to impress on order of the Gov'nor.

SEC. 2. *Be it further enacted*, That such impressment shall be made on the orders of the Governor, by the Sheriff of the several counties, any Sheriff failing to obey said order shall be punished, on conviction, by fine and imprisonment at the discretion of the Court; and the Governor shall, in failure of any Sheriff to obey said order, direct the duty to be performed by the Coroner or such other civil officer of the county as he may select, who shall be subject to the like penalties in case of failure.

All impressment of slaves to be made in conformity with this act.

SEC. 3. *Be it further enacted*, That no demand as (or) impressment of slaves or free negroes in the State shall be made, except in conformity with the provisions of this law; and if any shall be made in violation thereof, it is hereby declared unlawful and void.

Passed the House of Representatives December 3, 1864. Passed the Senate December 3, 1864. Approved by the Governor December 7, 1864.

CHAPTER 1,457—[No. 28.]

AN ACT to protect the Citizens of Florida.

Citizens arrested by Confed. officers.

SECTION 1. *Be it enacted by the Senate and House of Representatives of the State of Florida in General Assembly convened*, That whenever a citizen or citizens of this State shall be arrested by order of a Confederate officer, he or they so arrested shall be turned over to the Commissioner of the Confederate States, or the civil authorities of the county in which such arrest was made, or to the authorities of the county next adjoining for examination.

Officers failing to comply with the provisions of this act.

SEC. 2. *Be it further enacted*, That any officer who shall fail or neglect to comply with the provisions of this act, within a reasonable time after such arrest has been made, shall be guilty of a misdemeanor, and shall be liable to indictment before the Circuit Court of the District in which such offence was committed; and, if found guilty, be fined at the discretion of the jury.

Fees.

SEC. 3. *Be it further enacted*, That the fees and charges received in such cases shall be those now allowed by law in civil arrests.

Passed the Senate December 3, 1864. Passed the House of Representatives December 5, 1864. Approved by the Governor December 7, 1864.

CHAPTER 1,458—[No. 29.]

AN ACT for the relief of C. L. Demilly.

SECTION 1. *Be it enacted by the Senate and House of Representatives of the State of Florida in General Assembly convened*, That the Comptroller be and he is hereby authorized to audit and allow the account of C. L. Demilly, for services in cleaning and repairing arms in the year 1862, and the Treasurer shall pay the same out of any money in the Treasury not otherwise appropriated: *Provided*, That said account, or the amount to be paid thereon, shall not exceed such amount as the Governor may certify to be suitable and proper compensation for said services.

Comptroller to audit account.

Proviso.

Passed the House of Representatives December 3, 1864. Passed the Senate December 5, 1864. Approved by the Governor December 7, 1864.

CHAPTER 1,459—[No. 30.]

AN ACT to extend the terms of the Solicitors in the several Judicial Circuits in this State to the first day of January, 1866, and for other purposes.

SECTION 1. *Be it enacted by the Senate and House of Representatives of the State of Florida in General Assembly convened*, That the terms of office of the present Solicitors in the several Judicial Circuits be and are hereby extended to the first day of January, one thousand eight hundred and sixty-six.

Terms of Solicitors extended.

SEC. 2. *Be it further enacted*, That the term of office of Solicitors hereafter elected commence on the first day of January succeeding their election, and continue as now provided by law.

Commencem'nt of term.

SEC. 3. *Be it further enacted*, That the term of office of all State and County offices shall continue until their successors are qualified.

Terms of State and County officers.

Passed the House of Representatives December 6, 1864. Passed the Senate December 7, 1864. Approved by the Governor December 7, 1864.

CHAPTER 1,460—[No. 31.]

AN ACT in relation to the recording of deeds and other papers in Lafayette County.

SECTION 1. *Be it enacted by the Senate and House of Representatives of the State of Florida in General Assembly convened*, That the clerk of the Circuit Court of Lafayette county shall deposit in the Clerk's office, in Madison county, the books used

Books of record to be deposited in Clerks office of Madison Co.

1864.

Records. by him for the recording of deeds, mortgages and other papers of like character; and it shall be the duty of the said Clerk of the Circuit Court of Madison county to admit to record and to record in said books such papers as the law now requires shall be recorded in the said county of Lafayette, and that such record shall be as valid in law and equity as if the same had been recorded by the Clerk of Lafayette county.

Record books to be returned. SEC. 2. *Be it further enacted*, That whenever in the opinion of the Clerk of the Circuit Court of Lafayette county said books will be safe in his county, and he shall be able to resume his duties, they shall be delivered to him by the Clerk of the Circuit Court of Madison County.

Repeal. SEC. 3. *Be it further enacted*, That all laws or parts of laws conflicting with the provisions of this act be and the same are hereby repealed.

Passed the Senate December 1, 1864. Passed the House of Representatives December 6, 1864. Approved by the Governor December 7, 1864.

CHAPTER 1,461—[No. 32.]

AN ACT for the relief of Soldiers' Families.

Appropriation. SECTION 1. *Be it enacted by the Senate and House of Representatives of the State of Florida in General Assembly convened*, That in addition to the amount appropriated at the last session of the General Assembly, and yet unexpended, there be and is hereby appropriated the sum of Five Hundred Thousand Dollars. This amount to be disbursed in accordance with the provisions of an act entitled "an act to provide for the relief of Soldiers' Families, and others that require assistance," approved December 3d, 1863.

Officers to make quarterly returns. What returns made. SEC. 2. *Be it further enacted*, That it shall be the duty of the county officers having in charge the distribution of the fund for the relief of soldiers' families, to make quarterly returns under oath to the Governor of their proceedings, which shall contain a detailed statement of [the] number of persons receiving the benefit of this act, receipts and expenditures, and of distribution of funds entrusted to them, and also cause a copy thereof to be posted up at the Court House, or wherever practicable in their respective counties, and stating the wants of their respective counties, price of provisions, salt, &c., amount of provisions, supplies, &c., that can be purchased, and rates of transportation, and any other information that may be necessary to carry out the provisions of the act to which this is an amendment; and, in case of failure to do so, the Governor is hereby authorized to withhold all payments, under the act, to any county whose officers are in default, until such time as they comply with the provisions of the law.

Governor may withhold payments.

SEC. 3. *Be it further enacted*, That in addition to the duties required of the Justices of the Peace by an act entitled "an act to provide for the relief of soldiers' families, and others requiring assistance," approved December 3d, 1863, they shall assist the Board of County Commissioners, or Trustees of their respective counties, in the distribution of the funds and supplies which may be furnished them by the said Board of County Commissioners or Trustees, in their respective districts, under the direction of said Board of County Commissioners or Trustees; and the said Justices of the Peace shall make returns in writing, under oath, to the said Board of County Commissioners, as often as they may direct, of the manner in which the funds and supplies entrusted to them shall have been distributed; and in case any Justice of the Peace shall fail or refuse to faithfully discharge the duties imposed upon him by this act, and the act to which this is an amendment, he shall be guilty of a misdemeanor, and, upon conviction thereof, shall be fined not less than one thousand dollars or imprisoned not less than six months, at the discretion of the Court.

Duties of Justices of the Peace.

Returns.

Justice of the Peace neglecting duty.

SEC. 4. *Be it further enacted*, That any Judge of Probate, County Commissioner or Trustee, who has or shall hereafter assume the duties imposed upon him by this act, and the act to which this is an amendment, and shall fail or neglect to faithfully discharge the same, shall be guilty of a misdemeanor, and, upon conviction thereof, shall be fined not less than two thousand dollars or imprisoned not less than six months: *Provided, however*, That nothing in this bill shall be so construed as to prohibit the counties from receiving their pro rata share of the appropriation made last session and yet unexpended.

Officers neglecting their duty, how punished.

Proviso as to unexpended balance.

SEC. 5. *Be it further enacted*, That all laws or parts of laws conflicting with this act, be and the same are hereby repealed.

Repeal.

Passed the House of Representatives November 30, 1864. Passed the Senate December 5, 1864. Approved by the Governor December 7, 1864.

CHAPTER 1,462—[No. 33.]

AN ACT to define the duties of the Trustees of the Internal Improvement Board.

Trustees to make enquiry into rates and charges of R. R. Companies.

SECTION 1. *Be it enacted by the Senate and House of Representatives of the State of Florida in General Assembly convened,* That it shall be the duty of the Trustees of the Internal Improvement Fund to immediately make inquiry into the prices charged by the several railroad companies in this State for the transportation or freight of the citizens of this State, and especially the amount charged the soldier while traveling off duty, and which charge he has to pay individually, and to see that while full justice is done the railroad companies and their efficiency not interfered with, that the people are protected from exhorbitant prices, if they exist; and for this purpose the Board of Internal Improvement are hereby authorized to establish such tariff of prices for transportation and freight as they may be authorized by law and the charters of the companies to establish.

Trustees to establish tariff of prices.

Trustees to inquire as to employees of R. R. Companies.

SEC. 2. *Be it further enacted,* That the said Board inquire how many persons are employed on said roads, in what capacity, at what salary or compensation, and what are the several ages of the persons so employed, and that the Board cause the result of their enquiry to be published in some newspaper for the information of the public.

Passed the Senate December 5, 1864. Passed the House of Representatives December 6, 1864. Approved by the Governor December 7, 1864.

CHAPTER 1,463—[No. 34.]

AN ACT making appropriations for the expenses of the First Session of the Thirteenth General Assembly, and for other purposes.

Appropriation.

Senators.

SECTION 1. *Be it enacted by the Senate and House of Representatives of the State of Florida in General Assembly convened,* That the following sums shall be paid out of any monies in the Treasury not otherwise appropriated, to the following persons, to wit: To A. K. Allison, President of the Senate, $105 00; to E. J. Vann, Senator, $126 00; to James Abemcrombie, Senator, $364 00; to J. M. Arnow, Senator, $231 00; to J. D. Clary, Senator, $190 00; to J. C. Cooper, Senator, $225 00; to D. P. Hogue, Senator, $85 00; to D. P. Holland, Senator, $225 00; to Edw. Hopkins, Senator, $203 00; J. L. King, Senator, $217 00; to J. S. Russell, Senator, $106 00; to John Scott, Senator, $260 00; to W. J. J. Duncan, Senator, $141 00; to F. L. Villepigue, Secretary of the Senate, $556 00; to E. J. Judah, Assistant Secretary of the Senate, $380 00; to H. L. Howze, Engrossing Clerk, $380 00; to E. M. West, Enrolling Clerk, $380 00; to E. Bradford, Recording Clerk, $380 00; to J. White, Sergeant-at-Arms and Door-keeper, $530 00; to R. E. Frier, Messenger, $380 00; to Rev. E. L. T. Blake, Chaplain of the Senate, $100 00; to P. Dell, Speaker of the House, $253 00; to O. M. Avery, Representative, $364 00; to D. M. McMillan, Representative, $364 00; to James S. Baker, Representative, $134 00; to J. M. F. Erwin, Representative, $134 00; to T. J. Eppes, Representative, $225 00; to W. W. Brown, Representative, $182 00; to John L. Campbell, [Representative,] $190 00; to W. W. Poe, Representative, $155 00; to J. P. Atkins, Representative, $188 00; to T. D. Nixon, Representative, $105 00; C. E. L. Allison, Representative, $105 00; to N. T. Scott, Representative, $105 00; T. Y. Henry, Representative, $105 00; to R. H. Bradford, Representative, $91 00; to J. J. Williams, Representative, $85 00; to C. A. Bryan, Representative, $85 00; to J. W. Smith, $112 00; to R. Turnbull, Representative, $112 00; to J. Y. Jones, Representative, $100 00; to R. M. Moore, Representative, $98 00; to Thos. Langford, Representative, $133 00; to Chandler H. Smith, Representative, $127 00; to Robert J. Bevill, Representative, $155 00; to G. H. Hunter, Representative, $162 00; to A. Roberts, Representative, $168 00; to W. B. Ross, Representative, $162 00; to C. H. Davis, Representative, $325 00; to James A. Peden, Representative, $204 00; to J. A. Pacetty, Representative, $274 00; to Peter Monroe, Representative, $239 00; to G. M. Bates, Representative, $260 00; H. T. Mann, Representative, $260 00; to Elias Turner, Representative, $260 00; to Samuel E. Hope, Representative, $315 00; to H. L. Mitchell, Representative, $351 00; to R. W. Rutland, Representative, $380 00; to L. W. Odom, Representative, $302 00; to Jas. F. P. Johnston, Representative, $343 00; to Wm. A. Griffin, Representative, $393 00; to Wm. Woodruff, Representative, $320 00; to Rob. Wilkison, Representative, $344 00; to M. A. Knight, Representative, $175 00; to A. Cromartie, Representative, $98 00; to W. F. Bynum, Chief Clerk, $556 00; to A. J. T. Wright, Assistant Clerk, $380 00; to David Bell, Engrossing Clerk, $380 00; to W. M. McIntosh, Enrolling Clerk, $380 00; to F. M. Bunker, Recording Clerk, $380 00; to G. W. Floyd, Messenger and Sergeant-at-Arms, $530 00; to Genoa C. Townsend, Door-keeper, $380 00; to Rev. Dr. DuBose, Chaplain, $100 00; for general printing and publishing, to be audited by the Comptroller, $9,000 00; for printing laws and journals, to be audited by the Comptroller, in addition to the above, $4,000 00; to McDougall and Hobby, for stationery, &c., furnished the General Assembly, $530 00.

Representative.

Printing.

Stationery.

1864.

General Appropriation.

SEC. 2. *Be it further enacted*, That the following sums be and the same are hereby appropriated for the fiscal year, 1865: For salaries of Public Officers, $33,000 00; for Jurors and State Witnesses, $20,000 00; for Criminal Prosecutions and contingent expenses of the Circuit Court, $20,000 00; for incidental expenses Supreme Court, $600 00; for printing expenses Supreme Court, $1,400 00; for interest State debt, $30,000 00; for maintenance of Lunatics, $15,000 00; for residence of Governor, $1,000 00; for *Post Mortem* Examinations, $200 00; for Contingent Fund, $20,000 00; Clerk hire for the Executive, $1,500 00; for repairing Capitol, to be audited by the Comptroller, $2,000 00; Appropriation for stationery and candles, to be purchased by order of the Governor, $5,000 00; Incidental Expenses of this General Assembly, to be audited by the Comptroller, $400 00; Expenses preparing Treasury notes for issue, Clerk hire, &c., $10,000 00; Military purposes, $25,000 00,

Treasury notes to be issued.

SEC. 3. *Be it further enacted*, That, to meet the wants of the government, the Governor be and he is hereby authorised to have prepared and issued an amount of treasury notes not exceeding three hundred and fifty thousand dollars, in such form as he may prescribe, the public lands of the State to be pledged for the redemption of the same.

Bonds Confed. States to be disposed of.

SEC. 4. *Be it further enacted*, That the Governor be and he is hereby authorized to dispose of the Confederate States bonds and Treasury notes of all discriptions now in the possession of the State, upon the most favorable terms which can be obtained, and apply the proceeds, through the proper officers, to the payments required under the act of the General Assembly.

Passed the House of Representatives December 7, 1864. Passed the Senate December 7, 1864. Approved by the Governor December 7, 1864.

RESOLUTIONS.

---o---

[No. 1.]

WHEREAS, the Sheriff of Duval county, who was duly elected on the first Monday in October, 1863, has failed to give the bond required by law, and has been in the enemy's lines since February, 1864, and is still there, with no prospect of return—Therefore, Preamble.

Be it resolved by the Senate and House of Representatives of the State of Florida in General Assembly convened, That the election held on the first Monday of October, 1864, in the county of Duval, for a Sheriff, be held as valid in law as though said election had been regular, and the Governor be requested to commission the party elected. Election for Sheriff in Duval county.

Adopted by the Senate November 26, 1864. Adopted by the House of Representatives November 26, 1864. Approved by the Governor November 29, 1864.

[No. 2.]

JOINT RESOLUTION of confidence in and thanks to President Jeff. Davis.

Be it Resolved by the Senate and House of Representatives of the State of Florida in General Assembly convened, That the confidence of the people of the State of Florida in the ability, purity and patriotism of his Excellency, Jefferson Davis, President of the Confederate States, continues unabated, and that the able, fearless, and impartial manner in which he has administered the Government of the Confederate States demands and will continue to receive our approbation and support. Resolutions.

Be it further resolved, That a copy of these resolutions be forwarded by the Governor to the President and to the presiding officers of the Senate and of the House of Representatives of the Confederate Congress.

Adopted by the Senate November 28th, 1864. Adopted by the House of Representatives November 28th, 1864. Approved by the Governor November 30, 1864.

[No. 3.]

RESOLUTION of thanks to Capt. J. J. Dickison.

Preamble.

WHEREAS, Capt. J. J. Dickison, Co. D, 2nd Fla. Cavalry, by his high soldierly qualities and daring acts as a military leader, has challenged the admiration of the people of Florida and won their confidence to the utmost extent; and, whereas, Capt. Dickison has repeatedly defended and protected the people of Florida from the harrassing and destructive raids by the public enemy—Therefore, be it

Resolution.

Resolved by the Senate and House of Representatives of the State of Florida in General Assembly convened, That the thanks of the people of Florida are eminently due, and are hereby cordially tendered, Capt. J. J. Dickison and his brave command, and that we do recommend Capt. J. J. Dickison for that promotion he has so gallantly won and richly merits, and that the Governor be requested to have a copy of these resolutions transmitted to Capt. Dickison and his command.

Passed the House of Representatives November 24, 1864. Passed the Senate November 25, 1864. Approved by the Governor November 30, 1864.

[No. 4.]

RESOLUTION for the destruction of redeemed State Treasury notes and bonds of 1856 and 1861.

Redeemed Tres. Notes to be destroyed.

Be it resolved by the Senate and House of Representatives of the State of Florida in General Assembly convened, That the Joint Committee of the Senate and House on Finance and Public Accounts be instructed to destroy by fire the sum of twenty-six thousand seven hundred and sixty-two dollars and sixty cents in State Treasury notes redeemed under ordinance 49 and now in the Treasury office.

State Bonds to be destroyed.

Resolved, further, That said Joint Committees, in connection with the Comptroller, be required to burn and destroy $206,000 of State bonds of 1856, and $2,500 of the issue of 1861, according to resolution No. 8, of Dec. 3, 1863, the requirements of said resolution not being complied with for want of time by said committees at the last session of the Assembly.

Passed the Senate November 28, 1864. Passed the House of Representatives November 29, 1864. Approved by the Governor December 2, 1864.

[No. 5.]

RESOLUTION relative to relief for Soldiers Families.

Preamble.

WHEREAS, in the opinion of this General Assembly, the surplus provisions of the bonded men, which the county authorities are authorized to purchase from, for the support of soldiers' families, will not be sufficient, and agents of the Confederate Government have impressed the surplus corn of those farmers not bonded in many parts of the State, thus rendering it impossible for the county authorities, in many portions of this State, to purchase from them for soldiers' families—Therefore, be it

Corn impressed by Confederate Government.

Resolved by the Senate and House of Representatives of the State of Florida in General Assembly convened, That the Governor be requested to bring this matter to the attention of the Confederate Government, with a view of having so much of said corn so impressed released as will be necessary for the support of said soldiers' families, and authority given to the county commissioners to purchase the same.

Passed the House of Representatives November 26, 1864. Passed the Senate November 29, 1864. Approved by the Governor December 3, 1864.

[No. 6.]

RESOLUTION relative to the examination of the offices of Comptroller, Treasurer and Register of Public Lands.

Committee to make examination of offices.

Resolved by the Senate and House of Representatives of the State of Florida in General Assembly convened, That a joint committee of three from each House shall be appointed, whose duty it shall be, at some proper time before the next meeting of the General Assembly, to examine the offices of Comptroller and Treasurer and make reports as to the said offices, which are required by the acts under which they are organized.

Office of Register of Public Lands.

Resolved, 2nd, That it shall be the duty of said committee to examine into the condition of the office of Register of Public Lands, and report at the next session of the General Assembly all facts in relation to the affairs of said office which may be necessary to a clear understanding as to how its business has been and is being conducted.

Passed the House of Representatives November 29, 1864. Passed the Senate November 30th, 1864. Approved by the Governor December 3, 1864.

[No. 7.]

JOINT RESOLUTION requesting our Senators and Representatives in Congres to use their influence in procuring the re-enactment of a certain act of Congress.

Be it resolved by the Senate and House of Representatives of the State of Florida in General Assembly convened, That our Senators and Representatives in Congress be instructed and requested to use their best endeavors to have the present law, "providing for the establishment and payment of claims for a certain description of property taken or informally impressed for the use of the army," approved June 14, 1864, and which expires on the 1st of January next, re-enacted or continued in force during the war; and that the Governor be requested to forward a copy of this resolution to each of our Senators and Representatives in Congress.

Claims for property impressed.

Adopted by the Senate December 2, 1864. Adopted by the House of Representatives December 2, 1864. Approved by the Governor December 5, 1864.

[No. 8.]

RESOLUTION in relation to the rights of the States.

Be it resolved by the Senate and House of Representatives of the State of Florida in General Assembly convened—resolved, 1. That the States are sovereign in their respective spheres of action and under their respective Constitutions, and entitled to all the rights of sovereign States as such, and we recognize it as a fundamental rule of our government that all powers not expressly delegated to the Confederate States by the Constitution, nor prohibited by it to the States, are reserved to the States respectively, or to the people thereof.

Sovereignty of the States.

Resolved, 2. That the government under which we live consists of mutual checks and balances, which can only be secured by preserving the due separation and proper boundaries of the Legislative, Executive and Judicial Departments thereof, and the destruction or improper exercise of any of these three departments by either of the others is at variance with the Constitution and subversive of the true spirit of our free institutions.

Departments of Governments.

Resolved, 3. That the greatest liberty of speech and of the press, subject to the legal responsibility for the abuse of that liberty, the right of trial by jury at common law, the privilege of the writ of *habeas corpus*, the independence of the Judiciary, are cardinal principles of our free institutions, and it is amongst

Liberty of the Press and writ of Habeas Corpus.

the highest and most sacred obligations we owe to ourselves and our country to protect and preserve them *inviolate*, except in such contingencies as are provided for in the Constitution of the Confederate States for the suspending of the writ of *habeas corpus*.

Adopted by the House of Representatives December 1, 1864. Adopted by the Senate December 3, 1864. Approved by the Governor December 5, 1864.

[No. 9.]

RESOLUTION of thanks to our Soldiers.

Resolved by the Senate and House of Representatives of the State of Florida in General Assembly convened, That the thanks of the State are eminently due, and are hereby tendered, to Brigadier General Joseph Finegan, and to the troops under his command, for the signal victory achieved by them over a largely superior force of the enemy at "Olustee," in February last. Resolutions.

Resolved, further, That our soldiers, by their gallantry upon many hard fought fields, deserve our warmest praise, while challenging the admiration of the world, and Florida extends to her brave sons in arms the expression of her unbounded pride and thanks—pride in their prowess and patriotism, and pride for the noble deeds and undaunted bravery with which they have illustrated their State in many of the bloodiest battles of the war.

Resolved, further, That the Governor be requested to cause a copy of these resolutions to be sent to the several commands of Florida troops.

Adopted by the House of Representatives December 1, 1864. Adopted by the Senate December 2, 1864. Approved by the Governor December 5, 1864.

[No 10.]

JOINT RESOLUTION of thanks to the Citizen Soldiery of Florida.

Resolved by the Senate and House of Representatives of the State of Florida in General Assembly convened, That the thanks of the State of Florida are eminently due and are hereby

1864.

Resolution.

given to the citizen soldiery of this State, who so gallantly met the enemy at Marianna, Gainesville and other points in this State, and whose glorious conduct exhibited the highest traits of a brave and free people, and whose example is worthy of our emulation, and should make the people of Florida to be like them, always ready to aid the constituted authorities, State or Confederate, in the defence of our common country; and while the State of Florida mourns the death of her martyred citizens, and sorrows for her captive sons, yet she glories in the high fame acquired by their efforts and records their conduct among the brightest pages of her history.

Adopted by the Senate December 2, 1864. Adopted by the House of Representatives December 2, 1864. Approved by the Governor December 5, 1864.

[No. 11.]

JOINT RESOLUTION relating to the appointment of an Agent at Columbus, Georgia.

Agent for procuring supplies for soldiers' families.

Resolved by the Senate and House of Representatives of the State of Florida in General Assembly convened, That the Governor be authorized to appoint John D. Atkins as Agent at the city of Columbus, Georgia, for the purpose of procuring supplies for the soldiers' families along the Apalachicola river, and at Apalachicola, and to act as general agent for the State at that point: *Provided, however*, The said agent shall not receive any pay or compensation for his services.

Adopted by the Senate November 29th, 1864. Adopted by the House of Representatives December 1, 1864. Approved by the Governor December 5th, 1864.

[No. 12.]

RESOLUTION in relation to Mails in this State.

Preamble.

WHEREAS, the laws of the Confederate States now provide for a tri-weekly mail from Gainesville to Tampa, Florida, and there is but one mail per week for the present,

Request to have mail line established.

Be it, therefore, resolved, That our Senators and Representatives in Congress use their best endeavors to have said tri-weekly line established.

Be it further resolved, That a copy of these resolutions be forwarded to our members of Congress by the Governor of the State.

Adopted by the Senate December 2, 1864. Adopted by the House of Representatives December 3d, 1864. Approved by the Governor December 6th, 1864.

[No. 13.]

RESOLUTION in relation to destruction of redeemed Bonds of 1856 and '61 in Treasury Office.

Resolved, That the resolution relative to the destruction of 206,000 dollars of State bonds of 1856 and $2,500 of the bonds of 1861, be so amended as to read 293,000 dollars of bonds of 1856, such being the correct amount on hand in the Treasury office formerly hypothecated and returned by certain banks, as contained in Treasurer's report of 9th November, 1863. Amendment of previous resolutions.

Adopted by the Senate December 2, 1864. Adopted by the House of Representatives December 3, 1864. Approved by the Governor December 6, 1864.

[No. 14.]

RESOLUTION to relieve Archibald C. Black, Tax-Assessor and Collector for Gadsden County.

WHEREAS, it appears that Archibald C. Black, Tax-Assessor and Collector for Gadsden county, failed to comply with the provisions of the act of the last General Assembly, requiring him to make out three books in alphabetical order of all the taxable property in his county, &c., &c.; and, whereas, said failure was caused by the action of the Board of County Commissioners for Gadsden county, in not authenticating them, so as to be returned to the Comptroller's office in the time prescribed by law; and, whereas, further compliance with the law on the part of said Black was interrupted by his absence and duties as a member of a military company, which on several occasions was ordered out and marched to meet raiding parties; and, whereas, the books have been returned to the Comptroller's office properly authenticated and passed the approbation of the Comptroller, so that no material detriment has been done to the State or county, Preamble.

Be it resolved by the Senate and House of Representatives of the State of Florida in General Assembly convened, That the

1864.

Commissions to be allowed & fines remitted.

Comptroller be instructed to allow commissions to said Archibald C. Black, Tax-Assessor and Collector for Gadsden county, as provided for and prescribed by the law, and that all fines be remitted that may have been incurred by failure to comply with the requirements of the law.

Passed the House of Representatives December 3, 1864. Passed the Senate December 5, 1864. Approved by the Governor December 6, 1864.

[No. 15.]

RESOLUTION for the relief of the Tax-Assessors of Leon and Madison Counties.

Preamble.

WHEREAS, the Tax-Assessor and Collector of Leon county and the Tax-Assessor and Collector of Madison county did not file with the Comptroller their tax books for said county for the year 1864, at the time required by law; and, whereas, it appears that such default was owing to the failure of the County Commissioners and Probate Court to examine and certify said books, and not at all attributable to any negligence or refusal on the part of said Tax-Assessor and Collector in the discharge of their duty—Therefore,

Fines & forfeitures remitted.

Be it resolved by the Senate and House of Representatives of the State of Florida in General Assembly convened, That any fines and forfeitures that may have accrued, or to which the Tax-Assessor and Collector of Leon county and the Tax-Assessor and Collector of Madison county may be liable for failure to file or place in the office of the Comptroller their tax books for the year 1864, be and the same are hereby remitted, and the Comptroller directed to discharge the same.

Adopted by the House of Representatives December 3, 1864. Adopted by the Senate December 5, 1864. Approved by the Governor December 6, 1864.

[No. 16.]

JOINT RESOLUTION authorizing and requiring the Attorney General to print a General Index of the Decisions of the Supreme Court, and for other purposes.

Attorney Gen'l to have general index of the decisions of the Supreme Court to be printed.

Resolved by the Senate and House of Representatives of the State of Florida in General Assembly convened, That the Attorney General is hereby authorized and required to cause to be printed with the next volume of the decisions of the Supreme Court a general index of the decisions of said Court.

Be it further resolved, That the Attorney General shall also make an alphabetical and chronological index of all the statutes and ordinances of the State of Florida since the adoption of Thompson's Digest and now in force, designating any important amendments, embracing, as far as practicable, such matters as may be substituted for a digest or compilation, having reference to cheapness and efficiency; and for said services the Attorney General shall receive, upon the completion of the work, twenty-five hundred dollars, to be paid upon warrant of the Comptroller upon the Treasurer, and the Treasurer shall pay the same.

Attorney Gen'l to make index to the Statutes and Ordinances

Compensation.

Adopted by the Senate November 30, 1864. Adopted the House of Representatives December 2, 1864. Approved by the Governor December 6th, 1864.

[No. 17.]

JOINT RESOLUTION relative to the examination of the Treasurer's and Comptroller's office.

Resolved by the Senate and House of Representatives of the State of Florida in General Assembly convened, That the Joint and Select Committee appointed to examine the offices of Treasurer, Comptroller and Register of Public Lands, and to report at next session, be and they are hereby required to examine the Comptroller and Treasurer's offices, accounts and reports for the present year, and make a separate report as to them; and said Joint Committee shall be assembled at the Capitol, upon the call of their Chairman, and shall be allowed the same *per diem* and mileage for the time employed in the discharge of their duties as shall be paid while in actual session; and said compensation shall be paid on warrant of the Comptroller upon the Treasurer.

Committee to examine offices

Per diem and mileage.

Adopted by the House of Representatives December 6th, 1864. Adopted by the Senate December 6, 1864. Approved by the Governor December 7th, 1864.

[No. 18.]

RESOLUTION in relation to estates of deceased persons, orphans and minor children, and their protection from frauds.

Be it resolved by the Senate and House of Representatives of the State of Florida in General Assembly convened, That, whereas, it is manifest that the disordered state of the currency of the

Preamble.

1864.

country, growing out of the present war, has placed many of the estates of deceased persons in great jeopardy from the inordinate love of gain of dishonest and designing men, who have it in their power to defraud said estates, and also orphan children (and more especially those estates and those orphan children who are deprived of their legal and paternal guardians by being absent in the defence of their country) of their property by forfeiting bonds and other obligations given on a specie basis, and paying and discharging the same in currency at a greatly depreciated rate—

Judges of Probate and Solicitors to make report of cases of fraud.

Be it therefore resolved, And it is made the duty of all Judges of Probate and Solicitors of the several Circuits to report immediately such cases to the Judges of the Circuit Courts of the Circuits in which such fraudulent practices may have occurred, and that the Judges of the several Circuits shall have the matter herein provided for in charge and give it in special charge to the grand juries of their respective Circuits.

Circuit Judges to give special charge to Grand Jury.

Adopted by the House of Representatives December 1, 1864. Adopted by the Senate December 2, 1864. Approved by the Governor December 7, 1864.

[No. 19.]

RESOLUTION to ask that the Florida brigade in Virginia [be] sent to Department of South Carolina, Georgia and Florida.

Preamble,

WHEREAS, The Florida troops now in Virginia, commanded by Brigadier General Finegan, are weak and debilitated from bad health, from sickness and the fatigues of an arduous campaign, and in poor condition to stand the freezing weather of a Virginia winter; and, whereas, the strong probability of the invasion of the Southern coast of the Confederacy, that of Georgia and Florida; and, whereas, the Florida troops would be better able to endure the winter in a milder climate, and would also greatly recuperate their wasted health—[Therefore,]

Be it resolved by the Senate and House of Representatives of the State of Florida in General Assembly convened, That our Senators and Representatives in Congress be requested to urge the administration, if not incompatible with the public service, that said brigade from Florida be ordered to the Department of South Carolina, Georgia and Florida.

Resolution asking for transfer.

Adopted by the House of Representatives December 3, 1864. Adopted by the Senate December 5, 1864. Approved by the Governor December 7th, 1864.

[No. 20.]

RESOLUTION on Confederate Relations.

WHEREAS, in the re-election of Abraham Lincoln by the Northern people, they have pledged themselves to continue the war for the emancipation and arming our slaves against us, for the confiscation of our property, for the destruction of our homes, the murder of our citizens, the burning of our cities and the degradation of the white race and exaltation of the black race, Preamble.

Be it therefore resolved by the Senate and House of Representatives of the State of Florida in General Assembly convened, That all our sentiments and efforts towards peace have been spurned by the Northern people as signs of weakness on our part, we cannot consistently with our dignity and the interest of our cause, make peace propositions to them, but are, as we have ever been, anxious that this war should come to a close upon grounds securing our rights as a separate nationality. Resolutions.

2d. That we pledge our lives, our property and sacred honor to our sister Confederate States to stand by them to the termination of the strife, in resisting the army and government of the United States, and would prefer annihilation to remain with them.

Adopted by the Senate December 6, 1864. Adopted by the House of Representatives December 6, 1864. Approved by the Governor December 7, 1864.

[No. 21.]

RESOLUTION for the relief of William H. Durrance, W. S. Spencer and James J. Ward.

WHEREAS, William H. Durrance, Sheriff and ex-officio Tax Collector of the county of Polk, W. S. Spencer, Sheriff and ex-officio Tax Collector of the county of Hillsboro', and James J. Ward, Sheriff and ex-officio Tax Collector of Lafayette county, have been prevented by the condition and circumstances of the county and the hostilities of the enemy from making such returns relative to the assessment and collection of taxes for the year 1864 in their respective counties, to the Comptroller, as the law requires; and, whereas, it is unjust and improper to enforce the penalty of the law for such unavoidable default—Therefore, Preamble.

SECTION 1. *Be it resolved by the Senate and House of Representatives of the State of Florida in General Assembly convend,* That the fines and forfeitures which have or may accrue against Fines and forfeitures remitted.

1864.

said William H. Durrance, W. S. Spencer and James J. Ward, for failure to make returns as above stated, be and the same are hereby remitted.

Adopted by the House of Representatives December 5th, 1864. Adopted by the Senate December 6th, 1864. Approved by the Governor December 7th, 1864.

[No. 22.]

RESOLULION in relation to the Florida brigade, commanded by Brig. Gen. Finley.

Preamble.

WHEREAS, the Florida Brigade, commanded by Brig. Gen. Finley, in the army of Tennessee, has suffered greatly on account of the severewinters in Tennessee and upper Georgia, the regiments having become decimated; and, whereas, said brigade would be more efficient in a milder climate—Therefore,

Resolution asking for transfer of Brigade.

Be it resolved by the Senate and House of Representatives of the State of Florida in General Assembly convened, That our Senators and Representatives in Congress be requested to use their influence with the War Department to have the Florida Brigade, commanded by Gen. Finley, transferred to the Department of South Carolina, Georgia and Florida, and that Governor Milton be requested to forward a copy of this resolution to the Florida delegation at Richmond.

Passed the House of Representatives December 5, 1864. Passed the Senate December 6, 1864. Approved by the Governor December 7, 1864.

INDEX

TO THE

ACTS AND RESOLUTIONS

OF THE

First Session of the 13th General Assembly.

ADMINISTRATORS: (See Estates,) may file petition to keep estates together, 22, 23; may invest funds of estates in bonds of Confederate States, changing securities, 23; in military service, returns and commissions of, 25, 26.

APPROPRIATION: Act making appropriations for the expenses of the first session of the 13th General Assembly, and for other purposes, 32; Senate, 32; House, 33; General Appropriations, 34.

ARREST: Of citizens, (See Citizens of Florida,) 28.

ATTORNEY GENERAL: To make index of the statutes and decisions of the Supreme Court, 42, 43.

BENEZET, S., ACCOUNTANT: Comptroller to issue warrant in favor of, 14.

BLACK, ARCHIBALD C., Tax-Assessor of Gadsden county: Resolution for the relief of, 41.

BONDS: Of State, issued in 1856 and 1861, to be destroyed, 36, 41.

BREVARD COUNTY: County site of, 21; County officers of, 21, 22.

CARDS: Appropriation for purchase of cotton cards for distribution to soldiers' families, 27.

CASEY, ANNA L.: Administrator of estate of authorized to make title to certain lots in Columbia county, 25.

CATTLE, OWNERS OF: An act to amend an act for the protection of in the counties of Levy, Lafayette, Taylor, Wakulla and Duval, 15.

CENSUS: An act to provide for taking the census in the year 1865 in this State, 18; Tax-Assessors made takers of the census, 18; Enumeration of the inhabitants, list, returns, 18; Compensation, appropriation and forms, 18; Tax-Assessors failing to do duty, 18.

CIRCUIT COURTS: Judges of may hold extra and adjourned terms, 20; Governor may appoint or assign a judge of to hold Court in case of vacancy, 21; Judge failing to perform duty, 21; Compensation, 21; Western, judicial business of, 21.

CITIZENS OF FLORIDA: An act to protect, 28; Whenever arrested, shall be turned over to civil authorities, 28; Officer making arrest guilty of a misdemeanor if he fails to comply with the provisions of this act, 28.

CLAIMS, FOR PROPERTY IMPRESSED: Resolution asking Congress to re-enact law providing for the establishment and payment of, 38.

CLERK OF THE SUPREME COURT: Fees of, 27.

CLOTHING FOR TROOPS: (See Soldiers,) 26.

COMPTROLLER'S OFFICE: Examination of, 37, 43.

CONFEDERATE STATES BONDS: In Treasury of State, Governor may dispose of, 34.

CONFEDERATE RELATIONS: Resolution on, 45.

COUNTY OFFICERS: Governor may appoint in certain cases, 16; bond of, 17; in service of Confederate States, 17; election in October, 1864, 17.

CURATORS: In military service, commissions and returns of, 25, 26.

DAVIS, JEFFERSON, PRESIDENT CONFEDERATE STATES: Resolution of thanks to and expressive of confidence in, 35.

DEFENCE OF THE STATE: (See Public Defence,) 27, 28.

DEMILLY, C. L.: Act for the relief of, 29.

DICKISON, CAPT. J. J.: Resolution of thanks to and his command, 36; recommended for promotion, 36.

DURRANCE, WM. H.: Resolution for the relief of, 45.

DUVAL COUNTY: Election for Sheriff of declared valid, 35.

EDUCATION: Act for the education of soldiers' children, 19; list of children of soldiers, 19; County Commissioners to send children to school, 19; teachers, 19; accounts, 19, 20; Governor to control and direct schools, 20; tax, 20.

ELECTION LAWS: Law requiring ballots to be numbered repealed, 26.

EXECUTIONS: An act to amend the laws providing for the stay of, 24; soldiers not required to give bond under stay law, 24.

EXECUTORS: In military seavice, commissions and returns of, 25, 26;

ESTATES: Act in relation to, 22; may be kept together or divided, 22, 23; commissioners to determine division or not, 23; partition of real or personal property, 23; investment of funds of in non-taxable bonds of Confederate States, 23; widow entitled to wearing apparel, household goods, &c., 23; Resolution to protect from frauds, 43, 44; duty of Solicitors, 44.

FREE NEGROES AND MULATTOES: Impressment of for work on public defences, 27, 28.

FINEGAN, GEN. JOS. E.: Resolution of thanks to, 39.

FINLEY, BRIG. GEN.: Resolution asking that Brigade of be transferred to department of South Carolina, Georgia and Florida, 46.

FLORIDA BRIGADE IN VIRGINIA: Resolution asking that it be sent to department of South Carolina, Georgia and Florida, 44.

GUARDIANS: In military service, commissions and returns of, 25, 26.

IMPRESSMENT: Of slaves to work on the public defences, 27, 28.

INDEX: Of the decisions of the Supreme Court and of the Statutes and Ordinances of the State of Florida, Attorney General to make and publish, 42, 43.

JUDGES: (See Circuit Courts,) 20, 21.

LAFAYETTE COUNTY: Commissioners' Courts of, where may be held, 15; An act in relation to the recording of deeds and other papers in, 29, 30.

LAKE CITY: Corparate Limits of, 25; City Council of may appoint City Surveyor, Physician and Attorney, 25.

LANDS: (See Public Lands,) 24.

MAILS: Resolution asking for the establishment of tri-weekly between Gainesville and Tampa, 40.

MANATEE COUNTY: Courts and Public Offices of, to be held in the town of Manatee, 9; Act to consolidate the offices of the Clerk of the Circuit Court and Judge of Probate of, repealed, 9; Election of Clerk of the Circuit Court of, 9.

MILITIA: An act to organize Militia troops for the State of Florida, 10; Persons subject to Militia duty, 10; Organization to be preserved, 10; Officers and Elections, 10; Enrollment, 10; Other companies may be formed, 10; Persons failing to enroll themselves, 10, 11; Counties where no company organized, 10; Governor to prescribe rules and regulations for, 11; Battalions, regiments &c., 11; Subject to rules and articles of war when in the field, 11; General Court Martial, 11; Company by-laws, 11; Intemperance or bad conduct of officers or men how punished, 11; Patrol, 11; Arms and equipments, 12; Governor may order Militia to report to Confederate officers for the defence of the State, 12; Governor shall require return of the Militia as soon as the emergency for which they have been called out, shall, in his opinion, no longer require their services, 12; In case of raids or insurrection, 12; Persons over fifty years of age, 12; Company Courts Martial, 12; Exemptions, 12, 13; Militia Districts, 13.

OFFICERS: (See county officers) to continue in office until their successors qualified, 29.

PERRY, EX-GOV. M. S.: An act relating to the accounts of, 14; Comptroller to issue warrant in favor of, 14.

PUBLIC DEFENCE: An act in relation to, 27; Impressment of slaves for work on, 27, 28.

PUBLIC LANDS: Price of increased, 24; School and seminary, price increased, 24.

QUARTERMASTER GENERAL: To make estimate of expenditure, 22; Comptroller to issue warrant to, accounts of, 22.

REGISTER OF PUBLIC LANDS: Examination of office of, 37.

RUSSELL, WM. F.: Authorized to enter one hundred and sixty acres of land, 17.

SEMINARIES OF LEARNING: Judge of Probate of Leon county relieved from serving as member and Secretary of the Board of Education for, 19; Governor to appoint person to fill his place, 19.

SHERIFF OF DUVAL COUNTY: Election for declared valid, 35.

SLAVES: Special tribunal for the trial of created, 7; Tribunal composed of two Justices of the Peace, 7; Arrest of accused, 7; Notification and attendance of Justices, 7; Jurors and jury, 7, 8; Duty of Solicitor and Clerk of the Circuit Court, 8; Appeals, 8; Sentence, execution, umpire, 8; Slaves hiring their own time, 13; Impressment of for work on the public defences, 27, 28.

SNELL, H. V.: An act relating to the accounts of, 14; Comptroller to issue warrant in favor of, 14.

SOLDIERS, SICK AND WOUNDED: Act for the relief of, 16; Appropriation for, 16; Governor to direct expenditure of appropriation of, 16; Resolution of thanks to, 39; Citizen soldiers at Marianna and Gainesville, resolution of thanks to, 39; Appropriation for clothing for, 27.

SOLDIERS' CHILDREN: (See Education.) 19.

SOLDIERS' FAMILIES: Act for the relief of, 30; Appropriation for, 30; Returns of county officers, 32; Duties of Justices of the Peace, 31; Judges of Probate, County Commissioners or Trustees failing to do their duty, how punished, 31; Resolution asking surplus corn impressed by the Confederate Government for use of, 37; Cards to be purchased and distributed to, 27.

SOLICITORS: Term of office of extended, 29.

SPENCER, W. S.: Resolution for the relief of, 45.

STATES: Resolution in relation to the rights of, 38.

STAY LAW: (See Executions,) 24.

TAX-ASSESSORS OF LEON AND JEFFERSON COUNTIES: Resolution for the relief of, 45.

TREASURER'S OFFICE: Examination of, 37, 43.

TREASURY NOTES: Governor authorized to have issued, 34; Of Confederate States in Treasury of State, may be disposed of by the Governor, 34; Redeemed Treasury notes, to be destroyed, 36.

TRIBUNAL FOR TRIAL OF SLAVES: (See slaves,) Free negroes and mulattoes, 7.

TRUSTEES OF THE INTERNAL IMPROVEMENT FUND: Act to define the duties of, 32; To make inquiry into the prices charged by Railroad Companies in this State; Authorized to establish tariff of prices for transportation, 32: To enquire as to the number and compensation of employees on Railroads, 32.

WARD, JAMES J.: Resolution for the relief of, 45.

WIDOWS: (See Estates,) entitled to wearing apparel, household goods, &c., 23.